Angelika Schmelzer

Lungeing –
Be Safe and Proficient

Tips for safe and successful lungeing

CADMOS
EQUESTRIAN

Contents

Introduction 3

Safety first 4
Safety takes priority.........................4
The strength of staying calm 5

Equipment for lungeing 6
Equipment for the horse 7
Rein support 8
The lunge ring...........................12

Use of the equipment 13
Different goals, different techniques...........13
Correct use of auxiliary reins 15

Principles of work
on the lunge................17
The three phases of training.......................17
Communication between horse
and trainer 18

Correct training for
every horse 24
Lungeing young horses 24
Lungeing the riding horse 26
Lungeing as warm-up 27
Lungeing the rider 28
Lungeing over poles and cavaletti 29

Problems and solutions 31

Imprint

Copyright of this and original edtion © 2004
by Cadmos Verlag GmbH, Brunsbek
Design and setting: Ravenstein, Verden
Translated by Desiree Gerber
Projectmanagement: Editmaster Co Ltd,
Northampton
Photographs: Angelika Schmelzer
Printed by: Westermann Druck, Zwickau

ISBN 3-86127-946-0

Sturdy shoes and good gloves are advisable when lungeing a horse.

Introduction

Whether you ride or drive, besides work under the saddle, there are addidtional methods of working the horse on the flat that can be used.

The most common and also most versatile technique is lungeing on a single lunge rein, where the horse moves in a circle around the trainer. This basic principle can be varied, using different types of equipment and different techniques, and can thus be adapted to benefit every horse, regardless of its level of training. It can also be used by every rider who is prepared to acquire the appropriate skills. This versatility is best appreciated when the trainer is aware that there is no single way to lunge, but many variations that can be applied by the use of different combinations of all the techniques. The parameters of the variations naturally depend upon the individual capability of the horse, especially with regard to the reaction of the horse to the voice aids of the trainer, and other relevant factors. When deciding on a specific lungeing technique, not only must the question be asked as to the correctness of lungeing, but also about the level of training for each individual horse, as the trainer should also be considering the strengths and weaknesses of that particular horse.

The following accidents are not uncommon:

- A shying horse dragging the trainer, who has stepped into a loop of the lunge rein or got his hand caught in one of the loops that closed on the hand. In such instances the trainer can be seriously injured and even lose the use of a finger or sometimes the whole hand.
- The horse somehow got himself caught in the lunge rein, possibly through getting frightened and jumping sideways. He then runs away in panic and can stumble in the process, seriously injuring himself.

Most accidents can be prevented, and scary situations can pass without consequence, provided certain rules are followed. These rules include the correct use of equipment for both the horse and trainer and the way the trainer handles the horse.

Lunging can be adapted to suit any horse once the trainer is familar with the different technique.

Safety takes priority

Good, sturdy shoes and gloves are an absolute must when it comes to lungeing. Gloves prevent burn wounds from the rope and injuries to the fingers if a horse shies and suddenly pulls the rope through the fingers of the trainer. Sturdy shoes offer good footing and protect the trainer from bruised toes and broken bones in the feet through kicks or if the horse tramples on the trainer's feet. Clothing should be either zipped up or buttoned; nothing should flap around or rustle – as is the case when riding.

When accustoming a horse to strange or unknown equipment, the trainer must use a lot of patience; this is especially true when auxiliary reins are used, as these reduce the freedom of movement of the horse and can easily cause the horse to panic when used too early or fastened too tight. When leading the horse to the lunge arena the supporting reins should not be fastened at all! It is recommended that the legs of the horse should be protected with boots,

Safety first

When lungeing is done well, it is a highly effective and particularly gentle way of training the horse. The motivation of the horse can also be promoted when the necessary steps are taken for the safety of both the horse and the trainer.

Tendon boots , pads and bandage can keep the horse from injuring itself.

The strength of staying calm

The trainer must in all circumstances act in a calm and assured manner, in order to influence the horse in a reassuring way if dangerous situations come up and to prevent escalations of explosive moments. It is therefore important to practise certain movements, for example the holding of the lunge rein, carrying the whip and changing the whip to the other hand initially without the horse, until it becomes second nature. The way the trainer holds the lunge rein is of great importance. The rein needs to be held at the correct length, and with the help of the other hand the rest of the rein length is folded into big coils, one over the other. Great care must be paid to these coils. They should not be so big that the trainer can get caught in them by stepping through the bottom, neither should they be so small that the hand gets entangled if the horse suddenly tries to flee. The loop at the end of the rein must never be slipped around the wrist of the trainer; it must always be held in the fingers like the rest of the rein.

pads or bandages. This will protect the horse from strain, knocks, and overreach injuries. It is particularly appropriate if the horse has some kind of conformational fault or other anatomical shortcoming that can cause the horse to injure itself when working but it is of course also true of temperamental horses that can buck wildly and race around, injuring themselves through sheer exuberance.

The saddle or lungeing roller must be fastened tight enough to prevent slipping if the horse gets a fright and shies to the side. All equipment should be fastened in such a way that it does not flap around or slip during work at a faster tempo: stirrups must be taken up and secured and auxiliary reins, when not in use, should be rolled up.

The lunge rein must be held in such a manner that it cannot become tangled around the hand of the trainer.

A simple rope halter is sometimes sufficient for lungeing, but usually it will be the best for the horse to be dressed in his usual bit and bridle.

Equipment for lungeing

Different kinds of equipment are utilised to attain particular lessons or goals in work on the lunge. The most important tools are the lunge rein and the lunge whip. The best lunge reins are made of non-slip material and are around seven to eight metres in length. A loop handle sewn in at the end is not an absolute necessity: a thick knot can sometimes serve as a restraint if the rope is pulled from the hand. At the other end the lunge is hitched with a sturdy but not too heavy clip. The lungeing whip should have a strong, not too flexible handle with a long thong. The whole length of the whip, from the grip to the tip of the thong, should be around five metres; with this length the trainer will be able to reach the horse on any given spot on his body. A good whip must have a good feeling in the hand, must not be too heavy, and with a bit of practice, the trainer must be able to "snap" the thong.

Wrong: unstable and strong-acting lungeing . cavessons are not suitable for lunge work.

Nathe bits are recommended for use in lungeing.

Equipment for the horse

It is not recommended to lunge a horse dressed only in a head collar, even over a bridle. Even if you only wish to provide the horse with an opportunity to let steam off, it should be wearing a lightweight lungeing caesson.

The lungeing cavesson has a more intensified and therefore a more effective influence on the horse. The cavesson has a wide headpiece, similar to that of a leather head collar, with a strongly made frame over the nose. On the nosepiece a single ring is attached to the middle. There will often be two more rings on each side where the trainer can attach normal reins (when used for riding) or the auxiliary reins. Nosepieces made from metal only with jagged edges, often found in the Spanish varieties of the cavesson, are unsuitable.

The horse is dressed in his usual bit and bridle for work on the lunge. The reins are either removed or rolled in such a manner that they cannot sway to and fro. Curb bits are not suitable for lunge work and should be replaced with simple snaffle bits. Nathe bits have proved successful for lunge work and other forms of groundwork as they lie quietly in the mouth, do not tilt and are readily accepted by most horses.

*A crupper will prevent the roller
from slipping forwards.*

When auxiliary reins are to be used, a saddle or lungeing roller must be worn. Suitable lungeing rollers are made from durable material and are fitted with numerous rings: one ring in the middle on the withers, one at the deepest point on the girth, and at least three to four in between on both sides. When a lungeing girth does not have a cushion built in, some kind of padding must be provided. Many lungeing rollers have supplementary cruppers integrated, which help the lungeing roller to stay in place when the auxiliary reins pull forwards. When the horse needs to be accustomed to the saddle, or when it is being lunged prior to being ridden, it wears the normal riding saddle with the stirrups pulled high and secured in place with the stirrup leathers.

Rein support

Auxiliary reins are used in lungeing in the same way as reins are used in riding. It is often possible and even necessary to lunge a horse without the help of any auxiliary reins, especially when the use of these reins can lead to bigger problems. When auxiliary reins are used correctly, they can be of great help to the horse. All auxiliary reins have specific rules that need to be adhered to; these are described on pages 15–16.

The best-known auxiliary rein is the side-rein. Two reins, each with a hook on one side and a buckle on the other side, or similar fastenings, are hooked on the side of the lungeing roller and the ring of the snaffle bit on the same side.

Side reins are the most used, but not necessarily most suited.

Side reins with integrated rubber rings tend to teach the horse to lean on the bit via the "giving" rein, and should therefore only be utilised when the horse's mouth needs to be spared (for example when a beginner lunges for the first time). Side reins offer no stretch, they only make a bend possible. Used wrongly, they simply cause the horse to shorten his neck.

Lauffer reins, named after a dressage trainer, are a much better suggestion; unfortunately they are not yet widely available in the UK. An adjustable rein is hooked on both the inside and outside in such a way that a tapered triangle is formed. One end of the rein is hooked to the topmost ring on the side of the lungeing roller, the other end is then fed through the ring of the snaffle and then snapped to the lowest ring on the side of the roller. This auxiliary rein enables the horse to change his posture during the work on the lunge; in particular, a light forwards and down movement is allowed. The steady position of the rein in the shoulder area is also an advantage, as it offers the horse a good contact on the bit. This rein is appropriate for most purposes.

*The bend to the side is clearly seen
with the use of the Lauffer reins.*

At first glance draw reins look similar to Lauffer reins, but they have disadvantages. Draw reins come in two variations; they either have the same design as the Lauffer reins but get attached differently, or are in the shape of a Y, where the middle part actually divides into two reins at the sides. The end of the short, middle part, or the ends of the single reins are threaded through the girth, passing through the legs of the horse and dividing. The other ends are passed through the rings of the bit and are then hooked onto the rings on the side of the lungeing roller. These reins allow for a certain amount of stretch, but the horse can be positioned too deep. What happens then is that the horse comes behind the bit, falls on the forehand and moves with an inactive back and trailing hindlegs. The biggest failing of these reins is the absence of support on the outside.

The next three types of auxiliary rein all need an extra poll piece, which is added underneath the lungeing cavesson and has a ring at each side.

Both the chambon and the de Gogue consist of two parts. First of all, an adjustable loop is pulled through the girth and then passed through the front legs. On the front of this loop a ring is attached, and a thin rope with a snap link at each end is passed through this ring. The poll piece of both the chambon and de Gogue has two rings attached just below the ears. The snap links of the rope go through these and then are hooked onto the rings of the bit. The rope of the de Gogue follows the same route, but at the end the snap links are attached to the ring that passes through the loop between the front legs.

A chambon encourages the horse to
move in a longer, lower profile

Both these auxiliary reins promote a longer,
lower profile through pressure on the poll. They are
especially useful for horses with an extremely high
head carriage or a completely inelastic poll. The
chambon has a considerable effect on the mouth
of the horse and the de Gogue should be used in
preference. Both these auxiliary reins are unsuitable when collection is the primary goal of the work
on the lunge.

Finally the last auxiliary rein to be mentioned is
the check rein. This is a short, adjustable rein that
is hooked in the middle ring on the top of the lungeing roller. The rein then lies on the crest of the
neck and ends in a ring. From this ring there are
two ropes with snap hooks at the furthermost part.
These hooks get threaded through the rings on the
poll piece, from the outside to the inside and get
snapped on to the rings of the bit.

A ring attached to the bridle below the ears allows
the use of the chambon, de Gogue and check rein.

The check rein is often supplementary to side reins or Lauffer reins, and simply prevents the horse from evading the actual auxiliary rein, either from the side or moving down too far.

The combination of these auxiliary reins is better left in the hands of experts, for the influence these reins have on the horse requires due care and attention.

Use of the check rein should be left to specialists.

The lunge ring

An excellent lunge ring is a fenced-in circular area of not less than 20 metres diameter. This kind of arena provides safety for horse and trainer and helps the young horse by supplying a boundary to lean on at first. The ground surface should be non-slip, soft (but not too deep), easy to grip and must be flat. The track must be levelled on a regular base, for it can easily become hard, and deeper tracks can be created from the continuous work on the circle. The ideal track for the biomechanical function of the horse is when it has a slight slant to the inside.

When no lunge ring is available, a square area in the riding school or outside arena can be used. Free lungeing without a boundary is only advisable for advanced horses and trainers, and only then when there will be no interruption from any riders in the specific area where the horse is to be lunged.

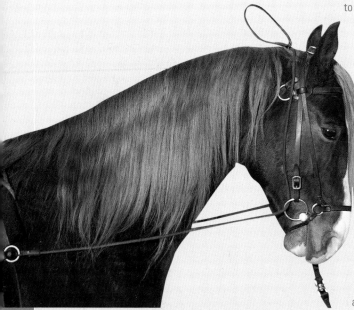

The halsverlenger is an unsuitable auxiliary rein. It is not widely available in the UK, in any event.

Lungeing with the cavesson alone allows for only limited correction of the horse.

Use of the equipment

Basic lungeing with a plain head collar and lunge rein as a practice round for beginners or for the horse to let some steam off, may seem a simple solution. However, if the trainer has gymnastic exercises or other objectives in mind, this kind of equipment alone is not sufficient.

Different goals, different techniques

The use of a cavesson and lunge rein means that there is a greater chance of influencing the horse. With the taking and giving of the lunge rein with the leading hand, the horse's head can be turned in the correct direction, that is, the direction of movement. When the horse is particularly flexible, the trainer can achieve a satisfactory level of work on the lunge through the use of only the cavesson and lunge rein. Major problems, however, cannot always be corrected in this manner.

The customary way of lungeing a horse is to put a bridle and lungeing roller on and then use a lunge rein and some form of auxiliary rein to work him. The lunge rein can be clipped to the bridle in a variety of ways:

• It gets clipped to the inside ring of the bit. The drawback: the trainer has a permanent pull on the inside of the bit.

• It gets threaded through the inside ring of the bit, taken over the poll and clipped onto the outside ring of the bit. The drawback: the lunge rein quickly pulls tight and then has permanent pressure on the bit.

When the lunge rein is hooked onto the inside ring of the bit, the bit gets pulled through the mouth.

Permanent pressure and tension is experienced when the lunge is clipped on in this manner.

When attached in this manner, the trainer has the same influence as when riding.

- It gets threaded through the noseband and the inside ring of the bit (for young horses).
- It gets threaded through the inside ring of the bit, under the chin of the horse and attached to the outside ring. The horse is then on the outside rein, as is the case in riding. The drawback: as soon as the slack is taken out of the lunge rein, the bit pushes onto the bars and gums of the mouth.

Due to these drawbacks, most riders and trainers prefer different ways of lungeing the horse. The following are of particular benefit:

- The horse is dressed in a bridle, lungeing roller and auxiliary reins plus a cavesson. The auxiliary reins are attached to the bit and the lunge rein is attached to the cavesson.

Auxiliary reins on the bit, lunge rein on the rope halter .

Advanced horses can be lunged without a lunge rein when a suitable lungeing ring is available. They are fitted with bridle, lunge roller and auxiliary reins and moved in the circle, with the voice, body language and lunge whip the only way in which the trainer can influence the horse. This manner requires greater experience and is not appropriate for every horse.

Correct use of auxiliary reins

In order to employ the auxiliary reins in the correct manner, the trainer needs knowledge, experience and sensitivity. Incorrect use of these reins can lead to problems with the training and safety of the horse, not to mention the possible accidents that can be brought about. Anyone who cannot deal with the difficulties of auxiliary reins should stick to the simpler way of lungeing the horse, on a cavesson.

When the horse is led to or from the lungeing ring, the auxiliary reins should not be attached. For the first couple of minutes, during the warming-up phase, they should not be attached either. Great care must be taken to secure them in such a way that the horse does not step on them.

As soon as the reins are attached for use, the trainer has to mind that the horse's nose stays in front of the vertical when the correct length is found. When observed from the side, the horse's mouth should be at the same height as the elbow (novice horses) or the point of hip (advanced horses) or somewhere in between.

Incorrectly attached, the horse goes behind the bit.

Many trainers prefer this way of attaching the Lauffer reins

The trainer must adapt the rein length according to the phase or the horse's level of training. It is often necessary to change the length of the reins a couple of times during a training session.

The reins are fastened at the same length, that is, the inside and outside reins have the same length at the beginning of a training session, or when a novice horse is worked. This causes the horse to stretch towards the bit with equal pressure on the reins.

When auxiliary reins are used that pass through the rings of the bit, there are two possibilities: the reins are threaded through either from the inside to the outside or from the outside to the inside. This differs from trainer to trainer and from the specific way the horse is being ridden; however, it is more logical that the first way mentioned above will make it easier for the horse to bring his nose to the inside and bend properly.

In principle the trainer should question the benefit and the moment in time any auxiliary rein should be used on a horse, and not blindly follow advice from outsiders.

The horse should let off steam and loosen up before any auxiliary reins are attached.

Principles of work on the lunge

The three phases of training

Every training session with a horse can be divided into three phases. At first the trainer starts to move the horse on the preferred rein, which is usually to the left. In the first part of the session, the relaxation and stretching or warming-up phase, the muscles are loosened and the circulation stimulated. Breathing and heartbeat are accelerated and the fluid around the joints reaches optimal temperature and consistency. In this first phase the auxiliary reins are not used. The horse is allowed to move freely in walk and will often stretch his head in the forward and down position. After about five to ten minutes the auxiliary reins are attached. The horse is now loosened further in the trot. Longer trot sessions may be necessary to let steam off more vivacious horses, or more transitions may be asked of their lazier counterparts in order to gain their attention.

Once the horse has been loosened on the easy side, the trainer asks for a change of rein. To do this the trainer asks the horse for a halt and then moves towards the horse, rolling up the lunge rein as he advances towards the horse, with the lunge whip pointing away. The horse is then turned on the forehand to face in the opposite direction and asked to halt again. The lunge rein is changed and fastened on the other side of the bridle. This all depends on the way the trainer prefers to lunge his horse.

In the working part of the lungeing session, auxiliary reins are used and the horse is collected.

The trainer then moves back to the middle of the lunge ring, slowly unrolling the lunge rein as he does so. The horse is then requested to work properly through stepping under his body again. More advanced trainers can ask the horse to work properly before being back in the middle of the circle.

Once the horse moves with cadence and rhythm on both sides and takes up contact with the bit, the actual training phase can begin. In this phase of the lungeing session the horse works towards collection, depending on the goal of the exercise. The trainer should have a definite idea of what he wants to achieve and at what stage he can make demands on the horse. During the working phase on the lunge, of about fifteen to twenty minutes, the trainer should change the rein at least once. At the end of the working phase the auxiliary reins should be undone and the horse should be allowed to stretch in a light trot in the relaxing phase. For the last couple of minutes the horse should move at the walk until the heartbeat and respiratory rate return to normal. The work on the lunge should altogether take not more than thirty to forty minutes, as the movement on a circle is a considerable burden to the ligaments and tendons of the horse.

Communication between horse and trainer

There must be a definite mutual attentiveness between the horse and the trainer during the work on the lunge, where different levels of communication are possible. This applies not only to the trainer giving signals to the horse as to what he should be doing. The horse joins in this conversation by the way he moves and the way he reacts to the signals from the trainer, thus conveying vital information concerning his strengths and weaknesses.

Young horses learn easier when the trainer uses body language to clarify something.

In exactly the same way as the trainer demands attention from the horse, the trainer should put all his concentration on the mutual work at hand, always ready to react in a flexible manner to the demands from different horses. In addition it is recommended that every rider should spend time observing his horse when it moves unrestricted in the paddock, in order to have an accurate picture of the natural movement of the individual horse.

There is more than one way to clarify different things to the horse:
• Using the equipment, especially the lunge rein and lunge whip.
• Using the voice.
• Using body language.

The trainer establishes his priorities according to the goal he aims to achieve and the level of training the horse is at. It is easier for the young horse to understand the voice commands and body language of a trainer. The more advanced horse will also have learned to interpret the aids given through the equipment.

The so-called spatial relationship, known as the lungeing triangle, is also of particular significance between horse and trainer. Seen from above, this tapered triangle is formed by the lunge rein, horse and lunge whip. Starting at the trainer, the connection between the hand and the horse's mouth form one long side of the triangle, with the hand with the whip pointing at the hindquarters of the horse forming the other long side of the triangle, and the body of the horse forming the short side of the triangle. The trainer must be approximately in line with the trunk of the horse. The trainer only leaves this space when he wants to indicate something with the help of body language or if he wants to move towards the horse in order to turn him around. Otherwise, the trainer stays on this spot in the middle of the circle, where he moves around as on a pivot.

The lungeing triangle contains the horse from the front and from behind while sending it on the circle.

The young horse more easily understands the trainer's body language asking him to increase the diameter of the circle .

As soon as the trainer moves away from this neutral position in the middle of the circle by taking a step in the direction of the movement, he is shortening the side of the lunge rein, and thus lengthening the side of the whip, and now ending up in line with the head of the horse. The horse understands this movement as a restraint and will automatically slow down his tempo, or even halt. Such an employment of body language is not customary in all schools; some adhere to the idea that the trainer should only leave his position in the middle of the circle in order to go to the horse. Using body language with the horse has one big advantage, namely that every horse is born with an innate understanding of this way of communicating. Young horses then find it easier to comprehend what is expected from them when the trainer uses body language at the beginning of their education.

The lunge whip is there to transmit forward and sideward aids – never to punish the horse. The whip replaces the driving leg and seat aids of the rider. The whip is held parallel to the ground with the end pointing to the hindquarters of the horse. Trainers will often, according to their own education, point the whip to the fetlock joint (for walk), the hock (for trot) or the croup (for canter) to indicate the different gaits to the horse. If the trainer performs this in a consistent manner, the horse can become particularly finely tuned to the aids.

A forwards driving aid from the whip comes from a swinging movement from the wrist of the trainer wherein the lash of the whip touches the hindquarters of the horse.

When the trainer aims to give a sidewards driving aid, the horse is touched on the belly or the shoulder with the lash of the whip. These subtle

The rein is held in this way.

This hold is recommended for strong horses.

aids with the whip, including touching the horse on the hock for more impulsion, require plenty of experience. The trainer should avoid waving the whip about in an uncontrolled manner, for this can either distract the horse, scare it or blunt his senses. The whip is not meant as punishment and should not be cracked under any circumstances.

When the trainer leads the horse to and from the lungeing area, the lash should be coiled or wound around the rod of the whip and carried in the left hand. When the trainer goes to the horse during lungeing, to fasten the auxiliary reins for example, the grip of the whip is lodged under the arm with the whip lying behind the trainer.

The lungeing rein replaces the reins and is used in a similar way. While at work on the right rein, the lunge rein is carried in the right hand and the whip is carried in the left hand, with the rest of the length of the rein looped in the left hand as well. On the left rein the lunge rein is carried in the left hand and the whip in the right. There are two ways the trainer may hold the reins: in the hand between the thumb and the index finger, or from underneath, from the little finger and coming out at the top of the fist. This last manner of holding the rein is recommended for strong horses.

A steady but elastic contact to the horse's mouth is what the trainer strives for when working on the lunge. Too strong or rigid a hand will dull the horse's sensitive mouth and disrupt its willingness to go forward. When the lunge rein hangs loosely, the horse cannot learn to search for the bit and the bouncing movement of the rein disturbs the mouth of the horse. If the trainer holds the lunge rein in a line with the horse's mouth, it is possible to give and take the rein in the same manner as in riding. Great care must be taken not to press the elbow into the side but to leave it relaxed at the side.

The wrist must be in a straight line, not bent or crooked in any way. The principle is the same in riding and in lungeing; rein aids should only be given together with driving aids, in other words the whip and voice aids!

The elbows hang loosely at the side, the lunge rein and whip are carried like this or as in the photo on page 5.

The voice aids serve as support for the commands from the whip, lunge rein and body language. Voice aids are also allowed in some forms of riding. These voice aids can in principle be employed to increase or decrease the speed at which the horse is moving, but also to change into another gait or move out to the track. The following are examples:

• A soothing tone in connection with a soft "hoo-oo", "brrr" or "shhhh" can pacify the horse in order for it to move in a more relaxed way.
• A vigorous tone in connection with an enthusiastic "come on" or clicking of the tongue can ask for more tempo.
• "Walk on" for the walk.

• "And trot on" for the trot.
• "Canter!" for the canter.
• "Halt" or "Whoa" to stop.
• "Move away" to move on to the track.

There are naturally many more voice commands that can be used as the trainer pleases. It is more important that the horse gets the message that the trainer wants it to move faster or slower, and that the trainer does not continuously change his tone of voice or command and make the horse unsure of what should be done.

Regardless of whether it is the voice, whip or lunge rein, all aids should be given according to the motto: as much as needed, as little as possible, in order to keep the horse sensitive to the aids.

When the driving aids are missing (whip) the horse will lose his posture and rhythm.

All the aids must have such a strong meaning in them that the horse will obey them immediately. In order to do this, the trainer uses his own deliberate intensity to issue a command: when the horse does not react upon a softly spoken aid, it must be replaced immediately with a more powerful version, and if the need arises, a third time with the use of body language. Body language often has an excellent effect and cannot be easily ignored by the horse. Driving aids are naturally used more often in order for the horse not to lose cadence, rhythm and posture.

The trainer must learn how and when to apply the aids. Should he want the horse to continue at a higher tempo, the trainer must:

• Give the appropriate voice command.
• Give with the hand at the same time.
• Drive the horse into the giving hand with the whip.

Should he want the horse to change into a lower gait, the trainer must:
• Combine the giving and taking lunge rein aids with
• a voice aid and
• a passive whip.

Similar aids are given when the tempo inside a gait needs to be changed: driving whip plus voice command and giving hand will increase the tempo, a giving and taking hand with a passive whip and relaxing voice aid will decrease the tempo.

A young horse should be able to find his own balance without the use of a bit or auxiliary reins

Correct training for every horse

Lungeing young horses

Lungeing plays a very important role in the education of young horses. It is used to establish the basic fundamentals:

• The young horse learns to trust its human counterpart and learns the meaning of the most basic signals.

• The necessary muscles to carry a rider are acquired.

• The young horse learns to carry a saddle and bridle.

• The lungeing is continued with a rider on out of safety for both parties and to create a smooth change from the known form of work – being lunged – to the new task – that of being ridden.

Starting a horse on the lunge is considerably different from the work with advanced horses and is best left to experienced trainers. It should be done consistently, with plenty of empathy and good sense in order to convey joyful cooperation between horse and trainer. The trainer should promote the horse's willingness to move forward and be attentive enough to nip bad habits in the bud before they can turn into big habits, for example when the horse changes the rein of his own accord in order to move on the "easier" side.

The first attempt on the lunge should take place without any bit or auxiliary reins, when possible only with a rope halter or lungeing cavesson

Lungeing the young horse with the rider on board prepares him for the task of becoming a riding horse.

until the horse can move in a more controlled and rhythmical manner and understands the most important commands. This process is made easier with a helper to support the horse the first couple of times by leading the horse on a lead rein on the circle. The commands of walk, trot and halt, are to be given by the trainer in the middle and the helper must then, if and when necessary, assist the horse in performing them. This is a guarantee that the lesson is learnt successfully. Soon the helper can unclip the lead rein and slowly move to the middle of the circle where the trainer can take over all command of the horse.

As soon as the horse moves forward in a good walk and a rhythmical trot and is able to halt on both reins, the first goal of training has been achieved. Now is the time to teach him to wear the lungeing roller and the bridle, all the while still lungeing the horse on the rope halter or caves-son. Only once the horse can wear the roller and bridle without any tension showing, can the auxi-liary reins be added. Great care must be taken not to attach the reins too short, for this might cause tension or even panic the horse. The horse must always be able to move forwards freely in the stretching phase, without any reins attached, and to stretch down his head and neck. Important ele-ments of gymnastic work for the young horse include many transitions, relaxing canter work and decreasing and increasing the diameter of the cir-cle. When all this can be accomplished without a problem, the young horse can get acquainted with the saddle and slowly be introduced to the weight of a rider.

*Working over poles strengthens the muscles
of the back and belly.*

Lungeing the riding horse

Lunge work with advanced horses can have
various aims. The lunge work can be employed:
• To bring variety in the training programme.
• To work at certain goals under saddle or to impro-
  ve upon them.
• To move young horses without the burden of
  weight.
The following contents of a lungeing lesson are
recommended:
• Transitions between different gaits and within the
  gaits: transitions as well as changing the tempo
  within a certain gait increases the activity of the

hindquarters. The horse moves in a good frame,
develops cadence, and becomes attentive and
relaxed.
• Changes in the diameter of the circle: if the trainer makes the horse move on smaller and bigger
  circles, the horse must bend his torso more and
  less, thus improving his suppleness. Slower gaits
  are suitable for smaller circles and bigger circles
  can be executed in faster gaits.
• Trotting poles: using trotting poles improves the
  movement of the back and the attentiveness of the horse.

  Work over the poles on the ground is normally
done in a working trot. Depending on what the horse knows, one to five poles are put in a curve to fol-

low the circle spaced the distance of the horse's trot steps. This is usually 130 cm apart for big horses. When the horse is more advanced, the poles can be moved closer together and raised to work on the collection of the horse, or placed on the ground with greater distances in between to work on the stretch and cadence of the horse.

Lungeing as warm-up

Lunge work is often employed to loosen tense horses under saddle before ridden work begins. This only has any meaning when it does not turn into an uncontrolled rushing around of the horse, which could just as well end up being the reason for the tension in the first place. Tension caused by over-training, bad riding, incorrect use of auxiliary reins or lack of movement due to the horse standing in the stable all day, will not be eliminated through lungeing alone. It is indeed completely practical to lunge some horses in the correct way before starting to work them under saddle, especially:

• young horses
• older horses or horses that are arthritic
• horses that do not concentrate well
• horses that are over-anxious
• horses that need to be corrected.

The lunge work should then be seen as an introduction and complement to the work under saddle, not as a means of tiring the horse and making it more easy to control through bucking and racing around.

When a vivacious horse is allowed to let off steam on the lunge ...

... it will concentrate better on the work that follows.

When the groundwork has been done properly, the rest follows without problem.

Lungeing the rider

There are two reasons to lunge a horse with a rider on: in the first place to get the horse accustomed to the weight of the rider and in the second place to educate the rider.

Young horses should always be touched on their backs and sides first as a preliminary experience. A helper holds the horse, the saddle is placed on the horse, the rider places a foot in the stirrup and jumps up and down next to the horse at first. The rider then places more and more weight on the stirrup and starts to put weight on the horse's back until he finally slides onto the horse's back completely. The horse is then praised extensively, the rider dismounts and the whole procedure is repeated several times.

If young horses are lunged to get accustomed to the rider, the horse should be lunged before the rider gets on until it is loosened up. The trainer then steps up to the horse where it stands on the circle, the stirrups are run down and the reins are attached to the noseband. The rider mounts and the horse is led on. It is not recommended to utilise any auxiliary reins at this stage, in order to give the young horse the best chance to find his balance under the new weight. Before long, the trainer can slowly return to his spot in the middle of the circle and lunge the horse as normal. Although the rider takes up the reins, he still holds on to the saddle and takes care not to disturb the horse. The rider does not have any influence with the reins at first.

Schooling the seat of the rider is also recommended for advanced riders.

The rider then gradually takes up the reins, one gets attached to the ring of the bit and the other stays on the noseband, and the rider works in synchronisation with the trainer, changing the aids from the trainer in the middle to the rider eventually. The next step is to unclip the lunge rein and for the rider to ride alone.

Riders that are beginners are lunged to learn to follow the movement of the horse without overtaxing them with the aids as well. Advanced riders can benefit from schooling of the seat on the lunge. In both cases the horse can be equipped with auxiliary reins to make it easier for the rider to concentrate only on the task at hand.

Lungeing over poles and cavaletti

The fundamentals of work with poles have already been explained. The horse should be provided with some kind of protection on all four legs when performing work over poles, be it bandages or brushing boots, and even overreach boots on the front feet. Auxiliary reins that support the forward stretch, for example the chambon or de Gogue may be used. All other forms of auxiliary reins must be applied wisely and definitely attached long enough so the horse can trot over the poles with a free, swinging back. The poles must be clearly visible and be an obviously different colour from the arena.

Cavaletti blocks open up many possibilities for pole work.

The poles must be secured with cavaletti blocks on the sides and may never be placed on the ground without any safeguard, for they are likely to roll away when the horse bumps against them. When a cross is built, it must be so low that the lunge rein cannot get hooked onto the sides. When work over poles is done, it is preferable that it is done in a riding arena rather than the lunge ring, this way the trainer can repeatedly shift the circle. As a warm-up the horse is lunged without the poles, then the circle is shifted to the side where the horse can trot over the poles. After a couple of rounds, the circle is again shifted to the original position. In this way the horse will not rapidly grow tired, which would only lead to accidents.

Here are a few ideas for placing the poles :
• a single pole
• four poles at regular distances from each other
• a row of poles with up to five poles in trot distances from each other
• up to five poles in a row, the middle one lifted slightly
• up to five poles in a row with the distance slightly more than the natural trot distance from each other
• up to five poles in a row, with smaller distances and all the poles lifted from the ground

Horses that are tight in their backs can be loosened with the help of pole work, but the incorrect use of auxiliary reins, for example, can make the situation worse rather than better.

Lungeing the horse over cavaletti and poles should therefore be left to a more experienced trainer.

Problems and solutions

When problems arise during lungeing, the trainer should first of all question his own way of proceeding and the equipment used. Many types of resistant behaviour stem from incorrect use of the whip, lunge rein and especially the auxiliary reins. Lack of obedience can often be attributed to either overtaxing – the horse does not understand the commands or is not yet capable of executing them – or to too little demand – the horse is bored.

The trainer should ask himself the following questions with every problem that occurs:
1.) Why does the horse respond this way?
2.) How can I rectify it?
3.) How do I prevent this from happening in the future?

The following problems often arise in lunge training:

The horse runs away in an uncontrolled manner

Vivacious horses often react with a joyful buck or two at the beginning of the training session or as soon as the canter is asked for; this can be tolerated without question. However, frequent, uncontrolled running, possibly in counter- or disunited canter, is dangerous for both the horse and the trainer and no meaningful work is possible. Likely causes for this kind of behaviour can be lack of movement (the horse is stabled all day), too much energy-laden feed, overtaxation, fear and pain. All of these possible causes must be considered separately and eliminated.

Run-away horses are lunged using both hands: one hand on the lunge rein as normal and the other hand on the loops of the lunge rein. When the horse then misbehaves, the trainer has more strength to control him. Horses hooked in auxiliary reins or horses running in counter canter or disunited can-

If there is no border around the lunge ring, disaster may ensue.

ter must be half-halted sooner rather than later. At the same time the trainer steers the horse towards the optical border of the lunge ring or moves sideways himself, into the direction of movement of the horse, for that in itself will act to convey disapproval. If the horse slows down, the trainer should shorten the lunge rein first before allowing the horse the forward movement again.

The horse stops, comes into the circle or turns around

This fault should, when at all possible, be corrected immediately in the movement in order to stop the horse from coming to the idea that this mistake is a break from the work. This fault often occurs on the more difficult and less preferred (often the right) side of the horse. When the trainer has a good connection to the horse via the lunge rein, in association with a consistent driving aid, this fault can often be prevented or nipped in the bud. Another solution may be that the trainer does not stay put in the middle of the circle, but walks with the horse at the point of the croup. From this driving position it is easier to prevent these problems. The trainer should, however, return to his position in the middle of the circle as soon as the situation allows it.

The horse is lazy

Laziness often appears when the horse is bored, is driven too strongly and thus becomes inured, when the auxiliary reins are incorrectly attached or when there is not enough variety in the lunge work. Lazy horses should not be lunged for more than twenty minutes, and this should include plenty of transitions. Work with poles can also be used as motivation, as long as the horse does not get tired.

The horse bends to the outside or the shoulder falls into the circle

In both these cases the fault lies with the trainer. Either the auxiliary reins are attached incorrectly or a rigid horse is lunged without any auxiliary reins. The latter is of course possible, but requires experience and a modified influence from the side of the trainer. When the horse is lunged without any auxiliary reins, the trainer should lunge the horse on a lungeing cavesson and consistently require the inside bend while at the same time applying a good driving force to loosen the horse. More promising is the correct application of auxiliary reins, making sure the horse's nose stays in front of the vertical and the contact is even on both reins, in a slight bend, in line with the direction the horse is moving in. However, when a horse is bent too strongly or too soon, it will only pave the way to tension through the body.

Well-informed lungeing takes place without showy effects, attaches great importance to safety and always questions the correct way each horse has to be worked, or wants to be worked. Then, and only then, can lungeing be an effective method of working the horse, improving both horse and trainer.

Well-informed lungeing brings horse and rider closer.